Is the Negro Making Good?

Or, Have Fifty Years of History Vindicated
the Wisdom of Abraham Lincoln in
Issuing the Emancipation
Proclamation?

By

CHARLES EDWARD LOCKE, D. D.

Author of "Freedom's Next War for Humanity,"
"Eddyism," etc.

Pastor First Methodist Episcopal Church,
Los Angeles, California.

ISBN: 978-1-63923-810-1

Printed: March 2023

Published and Distributed By:
Lushena Books
607 Country Club Drive, Unit E
Bensenville, IL 60106
www.lushenabks.com

ISBN: 978-1-63923-810-1

AUTHOR'S NOTE

The following discussion was delivered as an address to an enthusiastic audience of several thousand persons in Los Angeles, Cal. Because of multiplied requests, the author has consented to have it appear in this form for general circulation. The author has undisguised and affectionate interest in the colored people and their problems and prospects, and confidently believes that the Negro race is destined to realize the highest moral and intellectual and spiritual ideals.

The author is under obligation to the secretaries of the Freedmen's Aid Society of the Methodist Episcopal Church for urging the publication of this booklet. This great organization and similar societies in other denominations are doing more than all other agencies combined for the education and the elevation of the Negro.

FOREWORD

National salvation, like the saving of the individual, depends upon the ability to see and rectify mistakes. Slavery was a mistake. The Emancipation Proclamation began its rectification, but it did not finish it. The doing of that great task falls to-day on the sons of the freedmen, as well as on the former master class. Surely if those who suffered are doing their part, the Nation can not hesitate. This brochure attempts to show that, whatever else may be true, the American Negro at least is doing all that could be expected toward the final emancipation of America.

New York City.   W. E. B. Du Bois.

Is the Negro Making Good?

INTRODUCTION

THESE hurrying years are bringing us to an increasing number of centennial and semi-centennial celebrations of important events in the formative period of our National life. The first day of January, 1913, is most significant as being the fiftieth anniversary of the issuing of one of the greatest proclamations in all the romantic and thrilling annals of liberty. That providential act not only gave freedom to four millions of black people in America, but it was simultaneous with the freedom of more than fifteen millions of serfs in Russia; and was the initial step which resulted in the manumission of all slaves within the boundaries of all Christian countries.

Since this is one of the great chapters in "the Bible of the race that is being writ," it should not be unprofitable for us to inquire whether the subsequent history of these fifty years has fully vindicated the wisdom of Mr. Lincoln and his contemporaneous patriots.

While the avowed purpose of the Civil War

was to suppress a rebellion and dethrone the seditious principle of State rights, yet it was confidently expected by many patriots in the North that it would in some way result in the abolition of the slave traffic in America.

As the war progressed, Mr. Lincoln was repeatedly importuned to take the initiative and use his prerogative in declaring freedom to the Negro. He wisely kept his own counsels and waited for the leadings of the God of nations. When, in September, 1862, he was urged by a company of Chicago clergymen to precipitate his action, he replied: "I hope it will not be irreverent for me to say that, if it is possible that God would reveal His will to others on a point so connected with my duty, it might be supposed that He would reveal it to me; for it is my earnest desire to know the will of Providence in this matter."

President Lincoln had secretly registered a vow that when the Confederate army was driven out of Maryland he would then issue a proclamation of emancipation to the Negro.

When that event occurred, he called his Cabinet together and said to them, as he submitted a draft of the Proclamation to them: "Now I am going to fulfill the promise I made to myself and my God. I have got you together to hear what I have written down. I do not wish your advice about the main matter, for that I have determined for myself."

IS THE NEGRO MAKING GOOD?

"Of One Blood"

Athens was like an emerald in a setting of alabaster when Paul stood upon the flinty platform of Mars' Hill and made his incomparable appeal to the Areopagites. True, no Church was established in Athens as at Philippi and Corinth, yet an epoch was turned in the romantic history of Greece. The surges of a fretted paganism dashed against the rock upon which the fearless apostle delivered his challenge, but the restless waves reached that day their highest tide. The recession of Hellenism had begun; Solon and Plato ebbing into history; Moses and Paul carried by the flood of progress into places of imperishable power.

Among the startling propositions of the sermon which resulted in the awakening of Dionysius and Damaris was the statement, "God hath made of one blood all nations of men"—a matter much disputed before and since that eventful day, but manifestly a doctrine of Holy Scripture. Malachi speaks for a large company: "Have we not all one Father? Hath not one God created us? Why do we deal treacherously every man against his brother?"

With malicious persistence efforts have been put forth by materialism to invalidate Scripture by endeavoring to disprove and impugn the teachings of the Bible. But as in numberless instances the Bible has anticipated

9

science, so in this case. Because of striking physical likenesses, and analogies in language, the mental unity of men, and the manner in which the peoples of the earth are grouped, there is to-day a careful scientific deduction that man is not autochthonic, but that all the races of men have sprung from a central origin. For this position, Agassiz and Hugh Miller earnestly contended; and Cuvier, the eminent French ethnologist and founder of comparative anatomy, says: "We are fully warranted in concluding, both from comparison of man with inferior animals, and by comparing man with himself, that the great family of mankind loudly proclaims a descent from one common origin."

Certain ambitious authors and avaricious publishers are issuing books to-day in which a stupid attempt is made to show that the Negro is a beast, and not created in the image of God; that his place in the world is merely as a serving animal; and that Cain's great sin consisted in joining himself in marriage to a Negress. An improvident writer declares he spent $20,000 and fifteen years in producing such a book. It is, indeed, another instance of the mountain in travail. It is not heat and hot air that are needed, but light and truth. It affects to be a production harmonious with and based upon the Scripture, but it is with lamentable ignorance.

IS THE NEGRO MAKING GOOD?

The poet of the Psalms sings, "Ethiopia shall stretch out her hands to God!" Quaint Zephaniah prophesies, "From beyond the rivers of Ethiopia my suppliants, even the daughter of my dispersed, shall bring mine offering." Moses married an Ethiopian woman, and the Apostle Philip led the black premier from the realm of Queen Candace into the light, and baptized him in the name of Jesus Christ. All such attacks upon the Negro race are not only mischievous anachronisms, but they are unjustified and wicked characterizations.

Slavery Introduced

The Negro was brought to America by the "cupidity of commerce" against his will. Simultaneously with the landing of our Pilgrim Fathers on Plymouth Rock, a Dutch trading vessel, in 1619, arrived at Jamestown, Virginia, with a small cargo of black slaves. Cotton culture having commenced the same year, slavery rapidly extended. Some time since, in passing up the James River, I was remarkably impressed with the fact that, in its hurried rush to the sea, the impetuous stream is grinding away at the banks so successfully that already much of the site of Jamestown has been swept out of existence. A strange irony of fate—as if the genius of liberty were seeking for the effacement of even the desecrated soil on which mediæval tyranny pressed its defiling footsteps, and sought to establish itself in this land of freedom.

In 1776 there were in this country 300,000 slaves. When our National life began the feeling was strong against slavery. In 1787, when the ordinance excluded slavery from the Northwest Territory, some of the Southern States were even more enthusiastic than the Northern. In 1790 there were slaves in every Northern State except Massachusetts. In 1800 the number of slaves had reached 900,000. One by one the States in the North abolished slavery by gradual emancipation. In the South, however, because of the invention of the cotton gin, slavery became so increasingly profitable that there was some discussion concerning reopening the slave trade with Africa. In 1860 there were in the United States 4,000,-000 black people in bondage. To-day the Negro population is about 10,000,000.

To us to-day it seems incredible that it is scarcely more than a generation since Wendell Phillips found the following advertisement in a newspaper published in the United States:

"FOR SALE: A plantation—a library, chiefly theological books; twenty-seven Negroes, some of them very prime; two mules, one horse, and an old wagon."

IS THE NEGRO MAKING GOOD?

Steps were taken toward the abolition of slavery as early as 1775. About this time the Pennsylvania Abolition Society was organized, and it continued in existence until the manumission. Washington, Jefferson, and Madison opposed slavery, and in 1790 a memorial was sent to Congress, signed by Benjamin Franklin, asking that "Means be devised for removing the inconsistency of slavery." In 1820 the Missouri Compromise was effected. On January 31, 1831, William Lloyd Garrison published the first number of *The Liberator*, and sounded the tocsin, "Slavery a sin against God—a crime against humanity."

In 1844 the already great Methodist Episcopal Church split upon this inevitable rock, the Church of the North inditing with tears and prayers the memorable denunciation of slavery by its illustrious founder as "the sum of all villainies."

The Free-soil party was organized in 1848, and it sounded its battle-cry all over the land, "Free speech, free press, free soil, and free men;" and later, in 1856, when it nominated an impetuous Californian as its standard bearer, it added "Fremont" to its stirring motto. In 1857 there came the Dred Scott decision by the United States Supreme Court, which aroused the righteous indignation of the entire North. The Republican party was organized in 1856. Abraham Lincoln was elected

President in 1860. The Emancipation Proclamation was issued January 1, 1863.

The Abolitionists

It is inspiring to note how a group of men began to appear in widely separated parts of the country who were vehemently and unquenchably opposed to slavery. They were maligned and persecuted and wounded and ostracized, and some were killed, but still with unalterable purpose they persisted in a powerful propaganda against the evil.

The most fiery and pardonably immoderate of these was William Lloyd Garrison, a young Quaker. In 1829 he started a weekly paper in Baltimore, in which he advocated immediate emancipation as "the duty of the master and the right of the slave." He was soon convicted of libel against the owner of an interstate slave-ship. After forty-nine days in jail, he went to New England, and in 1831, in Boston, established *The Liberator*, the publication of which he continued until 1865, when it was considered to have fulfilled its mission. He is said to have been the most violently despised man in the two hemispheres. He was constantly threatened with assassination, but he never faltered. He said:

"I will be as harsh as truth, and as uncompromising as justice. On this subject I do not wish to think or speak or write with moderation. No! No! Tell a man whose house is on fire to give a moderate alarm; tell him to moderately rescue his wife from the hands of the ravisher; tell the mother to gradually extricate her babe from the fire into which it has fallen; but urge me not to use moderation in a cause like the present. I am in earnest. I will not equivocate. I will not excuse. I will not retreat a single inch, and I will be heard."

When Congress declared that it was prevented by the National Constitution from passing laws against the African slave trade, this fearless prophet denounced the Constitution, in the words of Isaiah, as "A covenant with death and an agreement with hell!" He and his compeers refused to vote for Federal officers, lest by so doing they might seem to acknowledge the Constitution, and one Fourth of July they daringly burned in effigy this historic document. When, in 1836, the Methodist General Conference favored not allowing the testimony of a Negro against a white person, he denounced that assembly as "a synagogue of Satan" and "a cage of unclean birds."

In 1835 Garrison was mobbed in Boston by "Five hundred gentlemen in broadcloth because in his paper he was damaging their Southern trade." These same "gentlemen" destroyed his printing press and scattered his types in the streets. But that day an extraordinary event occurred. As the young soldier and student, Saul of Tarsus, got his vision of duty as he stood by and held the clothes of the men who persecuted the first Christian martyr, so on that day in Boston a young lawyer looked out of his law-office window and saw the persecutors dragging William Lloyd Garrison along the streets by the hair. This young man had in his veins the bluest blood of New England, but his manly heart stoutly resented the unmanly and shameful manner in which Garrison was treated. He did not sympathize with the reformer, but he believed in fair play in the land of the free.

That day, with a heavy heart and with some new glimpses of duty, he returned to his home. His little invalid wife patiently awaited the coming of her handsome, gallant husband. As she sat in her cozy corner and he recounted to her the tragic scenes of the day, she tenderly, but with tones that were confident with heavenly wisdom, putting her arms about him, said:

"Wendell, you must take up the cause of the slave!"

The voice of· his wife was to him like the voice of God calling him to duty; and Wendell Phillips did take up the cause of the slave, and became the most renowned and persuasive orator of his time—a veritable

IS THE NEGRO MAKING GOOD?

Apostle Paul of Freedom. His stirring speeches were powerful in their persuasive logic. He did not resort to sarcasm and invective, but with finished and dignified speech he addressed the conscience and intelligence of this Nation. Only occasionally did he employ caustic utterance, as for instance, when, during one of his great speeches, he was disturbed by some callow youth who continually interrupted him, he stopped and, pointing to them, said, "Rotten before you are ripe."

A Martyr for Freedom

Time would fail me to tell in this connection of Elijah P. Lovejoy, a clergyman and journalist, who, like a Peter the Hermit, aroused all the Middle West with his fiery rebuke of slavery, and at last died as a martyr at the hands of a pro-slavery mob in Alton, Illinois, November 7, 1837, at thirty-five years of age; and of his brother, Owen Lovejoy, who took up the ardent labors of his fallen brother, and was afterward a member of Congress from Illinois (1857-1864).

Then, there was Gerrit Smith and Charles Sumner and Gilbert Haven and the eloquent black orator, Fred Douglass, who was born a slave, and his sable sister, Sojourner Truth. On one occasion, when Douglass was speaking with discouraged tones to a great audience, and expressed the fear that slavery might not be overthrown, Sojourner Truth, who sat on the platform, cried out:

"O Frederick, is God dead?"

O no, God was not dead; and the cries of the suffering, and the rich blood of the martyrs, and the sobbing prayers of the faithful all went straight up to the throne of the Eternal, and were to be answered when the fullness of time would come and a tyrannical Pharaoh would be willing to let the people go.

John Brown, of Ossawatomie

Then, there was the unique and eccentric John Brown, who made his stand, first in Kansas, in 1856, then at Harper's Ferry on the night of October 16, 1859. He who was the John the Baptist of freedom and who, on his way to his cruel but ecstatic martyrdom, stopped and kissed the beautiful baby of a grateful Negro mother. If the dome of John Brown's brain had been as lofty as his heart's sympathies were deep, there would have been another issue to his contention and his sacrifice.

On October 30, 1856, at Ossawatomie, Kansas, John Brown made his first stand for freedom and initiated a struggle which precipitated the Civil War and emancipated the slaves. That little battle, in which there were four hundred invaders from Missouri and only forty-two Free State defenders, was one of the victorious defeats of the history of freedom. Like the undaunted struggle of the "embattled farmers" at Concord bridge, so at Ossawatomie another shot was fired which was heard around the world.

John Brown said: "Providence has made me an actor and slavery an outlaw. A price is on my head, and what is life to me? I have a commission direct from Almighty God to act against slavery. Do not allow any one to say I acted from revenge. What I do, I do because of human liberty, because I regard it necessary."

Then, on October 16, 1859, there came the raid on the arsenal at Harper's Ferry, John Brown confidently believing that as soon as he would make a stand for the Negro, and furnish guns and ammunition, the slaves would flock to his standards; and they could easily fight their way to freedom, as did Spartacus and his fellow slaves in Rome long ago.

Fred Douglass once said: "Judged by itself alone, the raid on Harper's Ferry was a great crime; but it can not be judged alone. The cry that went up from the startled and terrified inhabitants of Harper's Ferry was but an echo of that other cry which began two centuries before the man-hunter first set foot in the quiet African villages. The raid at

Harper's Ferry was contracted for when the first slave-ship landed on these shores."

John Brown was a great man and a fearless and sublime hero. His death was as heroic as Socrates; and his speech in the courtroom at his trial, as Col. T. W. Higginson once said, is worthy of being placed beside Lincoln's Gettysburg address.

> From boulevards overlooking Both Nyanza,
> The statued bronze shall glitter in the sun,
>   With rugged lettering:
>   "John Brown, of Kansas—
> He dared begin; he lost, but losing won."

The minister who officiated at the funeral of John Brown, in company with William Lloyd Garrison and Wendell Phillips, was socially ostracized and compelled to resign his Church. But time is a just retributor, and in his old age, "Dr. Young, of Groton, Mass.," won great distinction and honor because of that event.

A Modern Deborah

In a Connecticut parsonage a baby girl was born June 14, 1811, who was destined to play an important part in the controversy against slavery. The atmosphere of that home of thirteen children was favorable to strong opposition to the crime of the century. The father was a tower of strength, a stalwart defender of righteousness, and an invincible and eloquent advocate of freedom. The mother, a beautiful and intellectual woman, died when the little girl was only four years old; so the child spent much time in the company of her father, and strongly imbibed from him his unyielding convictions against the curse of slavery and his affectionate interest in the black man.

When she was twenty-one years of age her father removed to what was then the far western city of Cincinnati; and later she became the wife of a cultured clergyman. In Ohio this sensitive young woman became familiar with the evil of slavery at short range. Over in Kentucky she saw a Negro child sold, and torn away from the arms of the fainting, moaning mother. Once a slave woman, with her child in her arms, fleeing for safety, had come across the angry, swollen river from Kentucky into Ohio, leaping from cake to cake of floating ice.

Then, in 1850, there was passed the atrocious Fugitive Slave law, giving to slaveholders additional facilities in recovering their runaway slaves.

All of these things deeply stirred the heart of this devout and patriotic young woman, who as the years hurried found herself surrounded with her own family of children and faithfully fulfilling all the many happy obligations of the true wife and mother.

IS THE NEGRO MAKING GOOD?

More than once she had expressed a desire to write something which would make the "whole Nation feel what an accursed thing slavery is," and in this she was sympathetically encouraged by her husband, who knew her brilliant qualifications.

At length, one Sunday morning during the service of the holy communion, as she worshipped in her usual place at church, there flashed upon her like a vision the picture of the death of Uncle Tom, a saintly old slave, and she seemed to hear the cries for help which came from the suffering Negroes, whose backs were bleeding under the blows of the cruel slave-whip. She burst into tears; and that afternoon, shutting herself in her room, she wrote a little story with a lead pencil on coarse, brown wrapping paper. Then, with her baby on her knee, she gathered her children together that same evening and read the story to them. One of her two little boys sobbed out, "O mamma, slavery is the most cruel thing in the world!"

The multiplied duties of her home caused her to lay the story aside, and she soon forgot it; until, at length, her husband discovered it. and she found him in tears over the brown wrapping paper. He earnestly advised her to make what she had written the climax of a serial story.

And so she arranged to furnish the story

to *The National Era*, an anti-slavery paper, published in Washington. It was begun in June, 1851, and was to continue three months. She was to furnish her manuscript in installments, but the story developed under the spell of her genius and was not finished until April of the following year.

An Epoch-making Story

As a serial story it attracted so much attention that there was a strong demand to have it appear in book form. Accordingly, in March, 1852, "Uncle Tom's Cabin" was issued, and within a year over 300,000 copies were sold. Its circulation rapidly increased in this country, and over one million copies were sold in England. It was translated in all into twenty different languages, there being twelve different translations in the German alone.

When the Italian translation appeared, the pope prohibited its sale—Infallible pope, ah me! And before 1856 it was dramatized in twenty different forms and acted in every capital in Europe and in all of the free States of America.

People read "Uncle Tom's Cabin" and sobbed and prayed, and cursed slavery. Many a man jumped to his feet and earnestly denounced the evil and registered a solemn vow that he would aid in its overthrow.

It was one of the first real guns that was fired against slavery, and it was fired by a woman.

Presses were kept busy running night and day. It moved adults to tears, and it entranced children and stirred them to patriotism. Many boys read the story early in the fifties and, ten years later, quickly and gladly enlisted to fight for the overthrow of slavery.

When some visitors, knowing how much occupied Mrs. Stowe must have been with her multiplied domestic cares because of her family of children, and the duties incident to a minister's wife, said to her, "How could you do it?" she reverently replied, "God wrote it!"

And why may we not all believe that God wrote it? The tearful tale passed far beyond her original thought. She did not know, when one installment was sent, just what would be continued in the next; and so, under the ministry of divine grace, this godly woman was used as a gracious channel by which God gave to the world the most powerful, epoch-making story of the century.

How Freedom Found the Negro

Freedom found the Negro utterly dependent, in a desolated land, without skill, property, or education. It also found him with distorted moral standards. What could he know of honesty and purity when he was accustomed to family ties being cruelly snapped asunder to suit the whims of heartless masters; and when the beauty and strength of his race were compelled to disregard all laws of modesty, purity, and marriage in order to propagate profitable chattels for their owner? Of course, the Negro had false ideas of freedom, and learned to his sorrow to stop singing:

> Farewell, hard work wid nebber any pay;
> I'se gwine up North, where de white folks say
> It's white wheat bread and a dollar a day.
> Look away! Look away!

Freedom also found the Negro, through no fault of his, with a great deal of Anglo-Saxon blood in his veins. If the Negro had not been emancipated, it was just a question of the calendar until the blood of the conquerors, which had been pitilessly mingled with his gentler nature, would manifest its historic character. The Anglo-Saxon is an empire-builder, an intrepid and imperious and assertive defender of his individuality. The future of American history would have seen the development of some resistless Toussaint L'Overture who would have led in a revolution beside which the story of Haiti's insurrection would have been child's play. This Afro-American is to-day demanding his rights—he is patient and submissive, but he has numberless friends, and let it be hoped that he will secure his equities, not by a revolution of blood, but by humane and Christlike evolution.

Some Good Slave-holders

In a discussion like this it is not only deservedly just, but an inexpressible pleasure, to pay tribute to the many good men and true who, though slave-holders, were upright and considerate in all their dealings with their slaves. So much was this the case that many persons of the South were righteously indignant when "Uncle Tom's Cabin" was published, and denied the truth of the chief statements of Mrs. Stowe's tragic tale until incontrovertible evidence was presented in support of the main facts in that epoch-making story. In many Southern homes the slaves were devotedly loved and sheltered, and when freedom was granted, many begged their old masters to retain them, even on the old conditions. At St. Louis Cemetery, in New Orleans, I saw that in not a few of the richly carved marble tombs some faithful slaves had found a final resting place side by side with the master and his family.

In that exquisitely pathetic little story of James Lane Allen, one reads with moistened eyes of the "two gentlemen of Kentucky." Black Peter's ardent devotion was no purer than the undisguised affection of the cultured

Kentuckian for his servant. "No one ever saw in their intercourse aught but the finest courtesy, the most delicate consideration. To be near them was to be exorcised of evil passions." This gentleman of Kentucky was typical of a large and honored class. He possessed "Southern sympathies, a man educated not beyond the ideas of his generation, convinced that slavery was an evil, yet seeing no present way of removing it, he had of all things been a model master. Often in those dark days his face, anxious and sad, was to be seen amid the throngs that surrounded the blocks on which slaves were sold at auction; and more than one poor slave he had bought to save him from separation from his family— afterward riding far and near to find him a home on one of the neighboring farms."

In this connection it must not be forgotten that many a worthy eulogium has been pronounced upon the faithful Negro nurses who helped to nurture the magnificent Southern citizen. One of these gentlemen, a business man of worth and distinction, in referring to his Negro "Mammy," said recently:

"Yes. You can not understand the love I bore for her. To her I told my troubles. When my father died, she comforted me. When I got married and came home with my bride, old Mammy was standing in the door in a black and white dress so clean and starched it would stand alone. She kissed my wife's hand, but she kissed my face. When the baby was born, she ordered me to step lightly, for 'Missus' was asleep. My wife died. But when she was buried, Mammy leaned on my arm and walked to the funeral. When it was over and I came from my room, she was holding the baby. She died not long ago in my house—and in my arms. You can not understand how I feel even yet."

When the friends of a certain centurion would persuade Jesus that the brave captain was deserving of His tender attention, they said of him, "He is worthy for whom He should do this!" The black citizen of the Republic has proven during the years of his emancipation that he is worthy of all that this generation can do to aid him in acquiring the position to which he is justly entitled.

The Negro's Progress

His progress justifies the hopes and prophecies of his liberators and friends. Congressman White, a colored representative from North Carolina, in a speech in Washington, reminded the Nation that the Negro is not what he was forty years ago. Illiteracy has decreased forty-five per cent. There are now 3,000 lawyers and as many physicians. His race now owns 200,000 homes and farms, covering an area of 38,000,000 acres, to the value of $750,000,000, and personal property to the amount of many millions of dollars. They are operating as cash tenants nearly 300,000 farms. This black statesman declared, "There is plenty of room at the top, and the colored man is climbing."

The Negro has much power of invention. Already nearly one thousand patents have been granted to Negroes. The first Negro who applied for a patent was a slave. He was refused, but it was afterwards issued in the name of his owner. The first machine for pegging shoes was patented by a Negro; and the fourteenth patent issued by the Patent Office after it began to number them was taken out by a Negro.

The Negro has already made notable achievements in music. He has a musical soul, and the folk-music of the old plantations and the recent eminent careers of Samuel Cole-ridge-Taylor, Will Marion Cook, and J. Rosa-mund Johnson justify the prophecy that America's greatest musician may yet be a colored man; and the elevator boy, Paul Lawrence Dunbar, has encouraged lyric lovers to look toward the colored people for some of the world's greatest poets.

Like the witty Irishman, the Negro has a fine sense of humor. I was stopping for a few days, some years ago, at the Galt House, in Louisville, Kentucky. My attention was attracted to a bright, handsome colored boy who took the hats of the guests as they entered the dining room. He possessed the remarkable facility of being able to return to each man his own hat without asking any questions. One day a dignified judge, who was holding court in Louisville, said to the boy, "How did you know that that was my hat?" And the boy answered, "I did not know, sir, dat dat was your hat; I just know, sir, dat dat was de hat you gave me when you went into de dining room!"

Did you ever hear the colored man's reason "why Adam sinned?"

> Adam neber had no "mammy"
> For to take him on her knee
> And to tell him what was right,
> And show him—things he'd
> Ought to see;
> I know down in my heart
> He'd 'a' let dat apple be,
> But Adam neber had no dear old "mammy."
>
> Adam neber had no childhood,
> Playin' round de cabin do'—
> He neber had no pickaninny life;
> He started in a great, big,
> Grown-up man, and
> What is mo'—
> He ueber had no right kind ob a wife.

The romantic achievements of the most extraordinary colored woman of our time, Miss

IS THE NEGRO MAKING GOOD?

Edmonia Lewis, reveals the latent possibilities of this long-oppressed people. Miss Lewis's masterpieces in sculpture and painting have won for her a permanent place with Harriet Hosmer, Hiram Powers, and W. W. Story. Her father was a Negro servant in the family of a rich man in Albany, New York, and her mother was of Negro and Indian parentage. W. O. Tanner has won notable distinction as a painter in two continents.

The Negro possesses an unusual gift of oratory. Within recent years Roscoe Conkling Bruce won the medal in a debating contest between Harvard and Yale, and was recognized by Harvard as her most gifted orator. This brilliant young Negro is the son of the late Ex-United States Senator Blanch K. Bruce. William Pickens, an Arkansas Negro, has also won the prize for oratory at Yale. There is no man in this country, white or black, who is more widely known and admired than Professor Booker T. Washington, the founder of the Tuskegee Institute. He is honored as a scholar, an orator, an educator, and a man of unusual sagacity and level-headedness—one of the brightest hopes of the Negro race to-day. He was born a slave.

There are scores of names prominent in Church and State which dislodge every argument against educational development of the

31

black man. Among these should be mentioned
Frederick Douglass, Senator Bruce (of Missis-
sippi), John M. Langston, Henry Highland
Garnett, Marshall W. Taylor, Drs. R. E. Jones,
J. E. Price, J. W. E. Bowen, I. Garland Penn,
Prof. Du Bois, and Bishops Robinson, Turner,
Gaines, Campbell, and Clinton.

Those choice words of Dr. Channing, written long since, have not been forgotten: "We
are holding in bondage one of the best races
of the human family. The Negro is among
the mildest and gentlest of men, singularly
susceptible of improvement, affectionate, easily
touched, and hence more open to religious improvement than the white man. He carries
with him, more than we, the genius of a meek,
long-suffering virtue." Legislation could make
the Negro free, but only education can make
him a citizen.

A Patriot

The Negro has been a worthy factor in all
the patriotic struggles of this Republic. He
fought bravely in the war of the Revolution,
and most nobly did he respond to General
Jackson's appeal in the War of 1812. General
Packenham's fine army of invasion, as it re-
treated forlorn and disastrously defeated, had
reason to remember the ferocious fighting
qualities of the Negro. After that historic
and phenomenal victory at Chalmette, General

IS THE NEGRO MAKING GOOD?

Jackson, addressing his dusky warriors, said:
"I expected much from you, but you have sur-
passed my hopes. The President of the United
States shall be informed of your conduct, and
the voice of the representatives of the American Nation shall applaud your valor as your
general now praises your ardor." In the
Mexican War again the Negro was conspicu-
ous; and in the greatest Civil War in the
world's history this black patriot fought, 186,-
017 strong, in 249 battles. Wherever responsi-
bilities were imposed upon him, he was a
valuable ally and a veritable black knight of
the flag.

The Governor of Massachusetts organized
the 54th Regiment out of Negro volunteers.
He then went over to Harvard College and
invited a noble young man to become its
colonel. At first he declined, and later ac-
cepted the trust. The regiment was assigned
to duty near the Confederate stronghold of
Fort Wagner. At length the order was re-
ceived to storm the fortification. The gallant
young colonel called his men before him, fully
explained the perilous and well-nigh impossible
task; and as he gallantly led the charge, he
shouted to his men, "We shall take that fort
or die there!" As one man that regiment fol-
lowed their brave commander. Up, up they
went, their eyes gleaming with courage and
anticipated victory. In a moment they would

turn the guns upon a retreating garrison, when suddenly there came a terrific volcanic erup- tion from the artillery of the fort, and the indomitable white colonel and the impetuous black regiment were all dead on the parapets of the fort. O, it was a merciless slaughter of consecrated heroes! And there to-day, in honorable sepulcher on the slopes of the hill, awaiting the bugle of the judgment morning, lies the dust of Colonel Robert Gould Shaw, surrounded by the men who with him won fadeless immortality in that victorious defeat at Fort Wagner. When Emerson heard the story, he wrote:

> So nigh is grandeur to our dust,
>   So near is God to man,
> When duty whispers low, "Thou must,"
>   The youth replies, "I can!"

And Saint Gaudens has achieved his great- est masterpiece in his immortal bas-relief which has made a corner of Boston Commons an imperishable shrine of American heroism.

Disfranchised

The enactment of certain laws practically disfranchises the Negro in many of the South- ern States. The shamelessness of this un- American legislation is only equaled by the attempt at justification made by Southern writers. It is claimed that the reason for the disfranchisement is that certain unscrupulous whites have manipulated the ignorant colored vote. Would it not be more in harmony with the traditional Southern chivalry to visit the punishment upon the guilty, unscrupulous white politician—upon the sinner—than upon those who are sinned against? It is a familiar problem, which was settled in ethics long ago, that "two wrongs never make a right," and this conclusion is as unalterably fixed as that two parallel lines can never meet.

A Georgian told, in my hearing, how in his town on election days hundreds of Negroes are employed on plantations or public works several miles from the voting places, with the understanding that the train will get them home before the balloting ceased. As if in good faith, an early start is always made, but when a few miles from the city the engine always breaks down and the train load of black citizens is delayed until after six o'clock, when the polls close. With sides shaking with laughter this "Georgia cracker," as he called himself, repeated, much to the amusement of those who sympathized with him, "Yes, of course it is strange, but the engine *always* breaks down!"

In response to this incident, a young man from North Carolina explained that in his State there was a law that all defaced ballots should be thrown out in the final count, and that those who presided at the polls in his city furnished to the Negro voters a defaced ballot, which the colored man unwittingly deposited, only to be deprived of his rights as a citizen.

Among the colored people of the South are already some brilliant legal minds; and as the Negro's head is developed in harmony with his tender heart and his giant body, he will contend logically and successfully for the rights which a domineering class are ruthlessly taking away from him.

Social Equality

The most vexatious element in this entire race problem seems to be the ghost of social equality, which bobs up serenely and is downed, only to reappear as imperturbable as before. That, however, is an issue by itself, and a wholly personal one. Social equality is no more a matter of legislation than intellectual equality. To accord to the Negro his political, educational, and religious privileges does not necessarily involve the question of social relationships. We do not consider a man our social equal because he is white, neither should we be compelled to reject a cultured man as our social equal because he is black. Social equality in all classes and coteries depends upon taste, culture, affinity, and environment. If either the Negro or the white man prefers to accord to his own race superiority and priority, that is his privilege so long as he does not interfere with the rights accorded to others by the Constitution. Mr. Lincoln said, referring to the Declaration of Independence:

"I think that the authors of that notable instrument intended to include all men. But they did not intend to declare all men equal in all respects. They did not mean to say that all were equal in color, size, intellect, moral development, or social capacity. They defined, with tolerable distinctness, in what respects they did consider all men created equal—equal, with certain inalienable rights, among which are life, liberty, and the pursuit of happiness."

If the aristocracy of New Orleans crowds Tulane Hall to listen to Professor Booker T. Washington tell of his theories and his demonstrations concerning his colored brethren, and applauds the cultured orator to the echo, and yet declines to receive this colored gentleman into their homes, who shall deny to them the right to choose who shall be the recipients of their cordial hospitality?

If, when he was governor, Theodore Roosevelt, when five of the leading hotels of Albany refused to admit as a guest Mr. Burleigh, the famous colored baritone of St. George's Church, New York City, who had gone to the capital to sing at a musicale; if the governor, when hearing of what he considered a gross indignity, cared to invite the talented singer to be his guest at the executive mansion; and if, when President, Roosevelt chose to entertain the foremost representative of ten millions of American citizens at a luncheon at the White House table; and if even fastidious President Arthur invited Mrs. Bruce, the wife of the colored senator from Mississippi, to assist at one of his New Year receptions, and she stood in the receiving line, graceful, modest, and intellectual,—it must be confessed that these are all matters of taste and preference, and it inheres in the right of each American to choose his friends without interference on the part of any who may not agree with him. This whole social controversy has been enlarged out of all proportion by the persistent projecting into it of a subject that is not germane. To render to the Negro his Constitutional rights does not and should not mean intermarriage and many other grotesque and impossible hobgoblins of miscegenation.

✓ A fair chance and fair play for every American citizen, white or colored, is all that is demanded. Roosevelt, when President, acted bravely and promptly, and was supported by millions of citizens, when he wrote concerning the appointment of Dr. Crum, an educated and upright colored physician, to a federal office in Charleston, S. C.: "I can not consent to take the position that the door of hope—the door of opportunity—is shut upon any man, no matter how worthy, purely upon the ground of race or color. Such an attitude would, according to my convictions, be fundamentally wrong. It seems to me that it is a good thing, from every viewpoint, to let the colored man know that if he shows in marked degree the qualities of good citizenship—the qualities which in a white man we feel are entitled to reward—then he will not be cut off from all hope of similar reward."

Doubtless there is great sympathy to-day in all sections of our country with Professor Booker T. Washington in his timely utterance before the Brooklyn Academy of Science: "Concerning my own race, I believe we shall make our most enduring progress by laying the foundations carefully, patiently, in the ownership of the soil, the exercise of habits of economy, the saving of money, the securing of the most complete education of hand and head and heart and the cultivation of Christian virtues. I can not believe, I will not believe, that a country that invites into its midst every type of European, from the highest to the very dregs of the earth, and gives them shelter, protection, and highest encouragement, will refuse to accord the same protection and encouragement to her black citizen."

IS THE NEGRO MAKING GOOD?

In New York, Professor Washington, in addressing an audience of colored people, said: "Eschew cheap jewelry. Quit taking five-dollar buggy rides on six dollars a week. Do n't put a five-dollar hat on a five-cent head. Get a bank account. Get a home of your own. Get some property. Get a start in the world in some way. What good is it to you Northern Negroes that you live in cities with paved streets, if you do n't own anything? Do n't be satisfied with the shadows of civilization; get some of the substance for yourself. Just as soon as you do, you will be recognized and encouraged, whether you are in the North or the South."

The late General John B. Gordon, of the Confederate army, who was a lover of colored people, used to tell this story. One day during the war General Robt. E. Lee met a Negro soldier, and said to him, "Where do you belong, Sam?" "O, I'se one of your soldiers, General!" he replied. "Have you been shot, or taken prisoner?" "No, sar," the Negro answered. "Well, I do n't understand that," said Lee, "for all my soldiers have been wounded or captured." The Negro rolled his eyes, and said, "O, I'se always back where de generals are!"

And the Negro belongs with the leaders, and as he is becoming educated he is more and more being recognized among the men of masterful minds.

Racial Prejudice

That man is no friend of this Republic who tries to arouse racial and sectional prejudices and antagonisms; and whoever seeks profit and notoriety by endeavoring to perpetuate differences which were settled in the chivalric struggles of the Civil War is a dangerous highwayman, and instead of having his bad logic and dangerous theories exploited, should be summarily suppressed. In reply to the ravings of such a mercenary literary guerilla and demagogue in an issue of the *Saturday Evening Post*, Professor W. E. Burghardt Du Bois, a distinguished and cultured colored professor, formerly of Atlanta, now of New York, in a subsequent number of the *Post* makes this caustic, concise, truthful, and logical reply:

"The thing that is worrying the South and the Nation is that, in spite of a tremendous handicap, past and present, there is slowly, steadily arising in this land a group of intelligent, thrifty, aspiring black men who demand and propose to have all the rights of American citizens. 'How is this righteous demand going to be met?' is the question of the hour and the greatest question before the American people.

IS THE NEGRO MAKING GOOD?

The South sends three answers to this mighty question. These are not its only answers, but they are the shrillest and most insistent: Tillman, the political answer; Vardaman, the economic answer; and Dixon, the social answer. 'Taxation without representation is democracy,' swears Tillman, and stands ready by force or fraud to tear up the very foundations of the Republic rather than let an intelligent black man vote. 'Train niggers to be serfs and servants!' shouts Vardaman, and stands ready to degrade labor and nullify the thirteenth amendment rather than allow any Negro to be more than his bootblack. And finally comes Thomas Dixon, shrieking: 'There's a black man who thinks himself a man, and is a man; kill him before he marries your daughter!' Fiddlesticks! Shame on a sane Nation for listening respectfully to such combinations of treason, brutality, and bosh! The Negro race is one of the great human races. American Negroes can not be colonized in Africa. All American citizens can be free and equal without danger to the Republic.

"In physical build the Negro is the equal of any and the superior of most human races; their primitive culture is the equal of that of any people—Germanic, Celtic, or Semitic; their higher culture has been shown in their contact with other nations, just as in the case of the German, who remained barbarians until Rome

42

taught them. So in Egypt, Ethiopia, the Sou-
dan, and North Africa, Negro blood has given
abundant evidence of the highest possibilities.
If it be objected that these were not pure
Negroes, it can be answered, 'Where are the
"pure" Germans or the "pure" Anglo-Saxons
or the "pure" Americans?' All civilized races
are mixed. Again and again the beginnings of
great civilizations have started on African soil,
and their failure in the last one thousand years
has been due to the same shameful Christian
slave trade that planted the 'Negro problem'
in America. Even in European civilization
black blood has been prominent from the day
of the fabled Negro brother of Parsifal to the
day of Poushkin the Russian poet, Dumas,
Browning, and Coleridge-Taylor. In America
the industrial, mechanical, and intellectual development of the land owes an inextinguishable
debt to Negroes, as shown by the careers of
black laborers, black soldiers, and black sailors,
not to mention Bannecker, the almanac maker;
Douglass, the abolitionist; Dunbar, the poet,
and our legacy of music and fairy tale.

"The Jews are not assimilated, because
they have the power to protect their daughters. And when Negroes have in law and
public opinion similar power to guard their
families from lecherous whites, there will be
far less amalgamation than to-day. If prominent Southerners, from Thomas Jefferson

down to some leaders of to-day, had found our black daughters as unattractive as Mr. Dixon alleges, there would not be two million mulattoes in the land as unanswerable witnesses to the truth."

If the colored man would come into his own in America, let him emulate the white man's virtues, but avoid all his vices, and take Jesus Christ as his ideal.

Did you see what old Uncle Calhoun Webster said: "When I sees a man a-goin' home wid a gallon o' whisky and a half-pound o' meat, that's temperance lecture enough for me—an' I sees it ehery day. An' I knows dat everyt'ing in dat man's house am on de same scale—a gallon o' misery to ebery half-pound o' comfort?"

The Crime of Lynching

In order to touch the entire field of the discussion which this address is expected to provoke, there should be some reference to the cursed crime of lynching. The viewpoint of a typical Southerner was presented by John Temple Graves, editor of the Atlanta *Evening News*, at Chautauqua, in August, 1903, in a characteristic address. He declared that Southern chivalry had glorified woman, and assumed that lynching was an expression of the Southern fixed purpose to defend womanhood. He said: "Lynching is a crime. It is anarchy. It is riot. It is a stab at the law. It is deplorable—appalling. But it is here. It is here to stay. Place here as the premise and postulate of your reasoning that lynching will never hereafter be discontinued in this Republic until the crime which provokes it is destroyed. This is a fact, not a theory. It is not as it ought to be, but it is as it is, and as it surely will be." He not only speaks apologetically, but approvingly, of "the mob as the highest, strongest, and most potential bulwark between the women of the South and such a carnival of crime as would infuriate the world and practically annihilate the Negro race." The best answer to these incendiary utterances is this statement from an editorial in the *Atlanta Constitution*, by Mr. Graves's cultured neighbor, Mr. Clark Howells. He says:

"The time when the lynching of a certain breed of brutes could be winked at, because of the satisfaction that punishment came to him quickly and to the uttermost, has given way to a time when the greater peril to society is the mob itself that does the work of vengeance. Against the growth of that evil the best sense of the Nation needs to combine and enforce an adequate protection."

Nor is it true, as is assumed by Graves and others, that lynching is for a "particular offense." In a study of reliable statistics, I have found that in a certain year there were thirty lynchings for murder, nine on account of race prejudice, two for incendiarism, one for slapping a child, two for miscegenation, one for passing counterfeit money, three for attacking white men, two for no cause, one for giving testimony, etc. In all there are nearly forty different offenses for which lynching has been the cruel and barbarous punishment. And, even if one should be disposed to palliate the crime of lynching when resorted to as a protection of a Nation's precious womanhood, this means of merited punishment should be abandoned and denounced because it is impossible to confine lynching to one offense.. It develops the spirit of vengeance, which leads to all the diabolism of the anarchistic mob. What was invented as a defense for Southern women must now be abandoned for their surer protection. As Justice Brewer, of the United States Supreme Court, said in July, 1903, "Every man who takes part in the burning or lynching of Negroes is a murderer, and should be so considered in the eyes of the law." The murderer is no friend of law and order and society, and lynching must be suppressed for our veritable self-preservation as a Nation; and Governor Blease, of South Carolina, is not a safe guide when he blatantly and shamefully advocates it.

IS THE NEGRO MAKING GOOD?

Deportation Chimerical

Wholly chimerical is the suggestion that there should be a separation of the races, and perhaps a deportation to Africa or somewhere else. The Negro is as necessary to the South as the South is necessary to him; and as the Negro is elevated by education and religion, he will become more and more indispensable to the North as well as to the South. Concerning this suggestion, Professor Du Bois says:

"To transport ten million human beings from America to Africa, provide for the disposal of their property here, and a proper beginning there, would cost at least $1,000,000,-000. There is no place in Africa open to colonization on such a scale; and if there were, how long would we be there before somebody's swaggering battleships would benevolently annex our gold mines? Moreover, we will not go to Africa; we are Americans, and right here in America we propose to fight out our destiny. I was born here, my father was born here, and my forefathers were honest, hard-working Americans two hundred years before the Dixons were dime-novelists. If Mr. Dixon is allowed the protection of the flag he fought against, surely I may claim the protection of that same flag which my fathers gave their blood to preserve in every war of the Republic."

IS THE NEGRO MAKING GOOD?

The Negro will never go back to Africa! He is here to stay, and without immigration from other lands, notwithstanding the lamentable ravages of the ills of freedom, he is holding his own in the increase of numbers with his white neighbors.

The Negro has as much right to America as the white man, and he will stay here.

One Negro met another and said to him, "'Rastus, I'se goin' to die!" "O, no!" said his friend. "Yes, sir, I'se goin' to die!" he repeated. "How do you know you are goin' to die?" "Why, de doctor says so, and he knows what he's givin' me!"

In all this "Back to Africa" nonsense the colored man knows what these quack doctors are trying to give him.

Education

Nor must it be concluded that the entire South is opposed to the education of the Negro. While the public schools of New Orleans refuse to carry the Negro children beyond the sixth grade, the Methodist Episcopal Church, South, has committed itself to the higher education of the Negro by the establishing of Paine Institute at Augusta, Georgia.

A cultured white woman of the South, whose parents and grandparents were slaveholders, has recently written, "Whatever the height of our own moral superiority, it must in God's eyes just measure the depth of our debt to the weaker race." After referring to certain shortcomings in the Negro character, she says: "Such matters should burden no one with a sense of the Negro's depravity. They spring from an undeveloped mental and moral consciousness. A few generations of reasonable patience and the Negro will have passed this trying point." These are golden words, and help to fulfill the claim of the silver-tongued Grady that the best friends the Negro has are in the South.

The God of nations has indissolubly bound together the black man and the white man; the future and the happiness and the power of each is involved, by a presiding Providence, in the well-being of the other. As Jesus Christ fell beneath the weight of His cross on His way to Calvary, a Cyrenian, in all probability a Negro, was seized and "On him they laid the cross that he might bear it after Jesus." Our age has laid a heavy burden upon a great portion of God's children, and it is certain that humanity's King will not be unmindful of their cries and woes. He reigns to answer their prayers, and to reward their devotion to Him in the hours of His unutterable passion. He has come into His Kingdom "to loose the bands of wickedness, to undo the heavy burdens, and to let the oppressed go free, and to break every yoke." The Resurrection Christ, as He hears and fulfills the petitions of His suffering children, will not forget the soul-longing of that black mother who, when seeking to have her son admitted into one of the Methodist schools of the South, said, in pleading tones, "I'se nobody, I nebber expects to be nobody, but I wants my boy to be somebody!"

Essentially Religious

The Negro is essentially religious—the religious side of him is all sides of him. There are now over 3,700,000 Negro Church members, who are shepherded by 35,200 ordained preachers in 35,000 church buildings. In the 35,000 Sunday schools there are 1,750,000 scholars, taught by 210,000 Negro teachers. These Churches give one-half million dollars annually to education, and are sustaining nearly 200 colleges, academies, and industrial schools. They are supporting over 100 foreign missionary stations at an annual expenditure of $50,000.

Professor Washington says he was once traveling through the black belt of the South, when he came to a little Negro cabin, around which many colored children were playing. Stepping up to a woman who stood in the door, he said to her, "Are any of these your children?"

"Yes, sar!" she replied.

IS THE NEGRO MAKING GOOD?

"How many children have you?"

"Sixteen, sar!"

Seeing a baby in her arms, he further inquired, "What is the baby's name?"

"Judas Iscariot!" the mother replied.

"O, my!" Mr. Washington answered, "did you not know that Judas Iscariot was the worst man in the Bible?"

"O yes, sar," she confidently replied, "I knows all about dat, sar. De Scripture says it would have been better for Judas Iscariot if he had never been born—and dat's just de way with dis baby!"

Fellow citizens, this Nation has a God-given trust. We must solve the problem which the presence of our Negro citizens imposes upon us. We of this age have inherited this great obligation, but the God of the races will help us to find that solution which will be for the honor of the white man and for the advantage of the black man!

Unpardonable and unjust discrimination is made against the Negro throughout the North in his practical exclusion from the skilled mechanical trades on account of the color of his skin. If this is not corrected by trades unions it will not be many years until the Negroes will form their own labor unions, and there will be sharp competitions in this country between white and black skilled workmen. If the Negro is treated fairly he will always be the friend of the white man. The Golden Rule, which is always color blind, can remove this stubborn obstacle in the way of the Negro's progress.

Doing What Can Not Be Done

Dr. Washington Gladden, in his "Recollections," says: "If the main thing to be done for the Negro is to keep him in ignorance and subjection, that is a task which requires no great amount of art—nothing but hard hearts and brutal wills. There is physical force enough in the Nation to hold him down for a while; how long that dominion would last I will not try to tell. The civilization built on that basis will fall, and great will be the fall of it.

"The moral law admonishes us not to make our fellow-man our tool, our tributary. 'Thou shalt treat humanity'—it is Kant's great saying—'ever as an end, never as a means to thine own selfish end.' Disobey that law, and the consequence falls.

"The stronger race that tries to treat the weaker not as an end, but as a means to its own selfish ends, plucks swift judgment from the skies upon its own head. On such a race there will surely fall the mildew of moral decay, the pestilence of social corruption, the blight of its civilization. This is not Northern fanaticism. It is a truth which has been uttered more than once, with the emphasis of conviction, by strong men in the South.

"'The best Southern people,' says President Alderman, of the University of Virginia, 'are too wise not to know that posterity will judge them according to the wisdom they use in this great concern. They are too just not to know that there is but one thing to do with a human being, and that is to give him a chance.'" Dr. Gladden quotes also the wise and noble words of President Kilgo, of Trinity College, North Carolina, on behalf of the Negro: "He lifts his dusky face to the face of his superior, and asks why he may not be given the right to grow as well as dogs and horses and cows. For a superior race to hold down an inferior one that the superior race may have the service of the inferior was the social doctrine of mediævalism."

With a considerable show of wisdom we say that the Negro, like the white man, must work out his own salvation; but we should co-operate with him in his colossal task. It is not fair to the Negro, nor is it any credit to the white man, that the National Bar Association has decided not to admit Negro lawyers; that some politicians degenerate into miserable demagogues in their treatment of the Negro; and that some so-called Christians treat the Negro as if he had no soul. Every man who is working out his own salvation has a right to a helping hand from his more successful brethren.

I acknowledge that is a herculean undertaking, but we must remember that General Armstrong, of Hampton, the tried and true friend of the Negro youth, used to say, "Doing what can not be done is the glory of living." Circumstances of civilization may have made the Negroes a backward race, but the brilliant present and the still more brilliant future will demonstrate that they are not a deficient people. An increasingly favorable environment will show that the black man has normal capabilities equal to other more highly favored races.

The Negro is Awakening

When Wendell Phillips saw upon the seal of a Southern State a Negro sleeping upon a bale of cotton, he asked, "And what will the people do when the Negro wakens up?"

The Negro is awakening—he is rubbing his eyes; let the white man not be asleep!

It is safe to predict that this awakening Hercules, if he is fairly treated, will never be a menace to this Republic—he will prove himself a friend tried and true to the flag, under whose soft folds he was nursed into freedom. And perhaps in some unpropitious future day, when foreign foes or domestic traitors shall assault the strongholds of American liberty and our citadels of security shall be tottering before a mighty, malicious giant, there will march up from the bayous and savannahs of the Southland a multitudinous army of black patriots whose chivalry and devotion may save our Nation in the hour of its great peril and emergency.

The Negro naturally possesses to some degree all the qualities of true manliness. He has shown himself an orator of fervid and impassioned eloquence. He is a lover of music, and has sung the chivalry of the South to sleep with his lullabys and has enchanted the world with his mellifluous melodies.

He has been true to the sacred trusts imposed upon him. Henry W. Grady, Georgia's most eloquent and distinguished citizen, told thrillingly of the Negro's fidelity, declaring that there is not an instance on record of a single black man violating his master's trust during that long civil conflict when the Southern men were at the front fighting for their convictions, and had left their wives and daughters and property in the care of their trusted servants; and referring to his mother, from whom he had to be separated, he said, "I thank God that she is safe in her sanctuary, because her slaves, sentinel in the silent cabin, or guard at her chamber door, put a black man's loyalty between her and danger."

Although our people are lamentably slow

in giving to the colored man his just recognition, and guilty in some directions of criminal neglect, yet America, according to Sir Harry Johnston, of Great Britain, who has been for years an administrator over Negro affairs in Africa, is the best place on the globe for the black man.

We must not forget, as Dr. J. W. E. Bowen eloquently says, that the Negro has passed only fifty milestones since "he walked out from slavery with the chains broken, but not off, clanking about and clinging to his manly limbs, his wife under one arm, his child under the other, with empty hands, but with a buoyancy of heart and a lightness of tread and a freedom from revenge that made the world stop and wonder, and with faith in his God and his own destiny, he went to work, built himself a house, bought a farm, erected a bank, invested in stock, and through the schoolhouse and the power of the gospel erected a family altar, and is now making home, the fallen sister of heaven, his paradise for the rearing of his children and the joy of his heart."

His Faith in God

The Negro has indeed a strong intuitive religious nature, which is already reaching the highest Christian altitudes. Their religion helped to make them tractable and contented in all the ordeals and tortures of slavery, and is helping to make them patient in the tardy realizations of freedom.

A slave mother, who was forced to go before daybreak each morning to work in the swamps, would leave some breakfast for her two little boys, who were still sleeping on the straw in a corner. She would be gone all day, and before she returned at night the tired, lonesome little fellows would curl themselves up in the straw and go to sleep. When she returned she would cook a supper and, awaking the boys, they would have their only meal together. Then the mother would kneel in prayer with her arms about her little boys; and she would pray for the overthrow of the infamous institution of slavery, that her two boys might be freemen, and have a chance to make a character in the world; and as she prayed, her mother-tears would fall like rain upon the upturned faces of her two sons. God heard that mother's prayer—and one of her boys, as a Christian minister, graphically described this tender scene.

When Sumter was fired upon, somebody threatened to tear down the Stars and Stripes, which floated above a newspaper office in Richmond. The old Negro janitor endangered his life when night came on by ascending to the flagstaff and rescuing the holy symbol of liberty. He took it home, and his resourceful wife hid it away in a bedtick in their little spare room; and many a time during the long war they would go where it was and on their knees implore High Heaven to give victory to the flag and save the land from sedition and disruption.

Dar's a white man knockin' at de cabin do'!
    Don' you let de white man in!
He lookin' mighty weary an' he lookin' mighty pore,
    Don' you let de white man in!
He lookin' mighty hungry, an' de bacon gettin' low,
De meal am gettin' sca'cer, an' de yams don' grow;
How we gwine to get a libin' dis yer nigga' don' know!
    Don' you let de white man in!

Jus' step up to de do' an' tell him go away,
    Don' you let de white man in!
He lookin' mighty weary, an' I know he want to stay,
    Don' you let de white man in!
Wha' dat de white man muttah? He's a Lincum soger man?
He jus' 'scape from de rebels, an' dey cotch him if dey can?
Jes' hurry up dar, Dinah! Get de bacon in de pan!
    Come in, Lincum soger! Come in!

Make de hoe-cake ready! Make de fiah burn up high!
    Come in, Lincum soger! Come in!
'Fo' de rebels take you back dis yer nigga' shuah he'll die!
    Come in, Lincum soger! Come in!
De houn's on yo' track? I can tu'n dem from de do'!
Jus' pull off you' shoes; I fool de pesky houn's befo'!
I can lead de dawgs away—dey won't come back no mo'!
    Come in, Lincum soger! Come in!

IS THE NEGRO MAKING GOOD?

Jus' clim' up in de loft 'n' pull de ladder froo de hole!
   Lay low, Lincum soger! Lay low!
Put de trap-do' down 'n' keep as quiet as a mole,
   Lay low, Lincum soger! Lay low!
Now, Dinah! fool de rebels; say you dribe de man
 away,
But keep dem here a-jawin' jus' as long as dey will
 stay.
My Lawd! I must be runnin'! Don' yo' heah de houn's
 bay?
   Pray ha'd, Lincum soger! Pray ha'd!
    * * * * *

Now, praise de bressed Lawd! for de soger man am
 save!
   Come down, Lincum soger! Come down!
Dis nigga' made a straight line for de wi'ches' "Black
 hole cave."
   Come down, Lincum soger! Come down!
I pull off yo' shoes an' I drap 'm down de hole,
Den rub my feet wid sas'fras, an' clim' up on de knoll,
An' sit down dere an' larf, an' mak' my eye-balls roll.
  · Yah-ya! Lincum soger, yah-ya!

De houn's came a-bayin' an' dey run up to de cave;
   Yah-ya! Lincum soger, yah-ya!
De rebels came a-ridin', an' dey cuss an' sw'ar an' rave;
   Yah-ya! Lincum soger, yah-ya!
I tole dem you jump in, an' dat yo' goin' down dare yit,
Cayse de black hole cave, dey say, am "a bottomless pit."
My! how de cap'n cuss an' rave! I thought he have
 a fit!
   Yah-ya! Lincum soger, yah-ya!

Make de hoe-cake ready! Make de fiah bu'n up high!
   Praise de Lawd, Lincum soger! Praise de Lawd!
'Fo' de rebels take you back dis yer' nigga' shuah he
 die!
   Praise de Lawd, Lincum soger! Praise de Lawd!

IS THE NEGRO MAKING GOOD?

Befo' sun-up I will lead you to de Lincum soger camp;
But we mus' be movin' airly fo'ts a' right sma't tramp.
Eat a b'a'ty meal, young soger, for de night am cole
    an' damp.
     He'p yo'se'f, Lincum soger! He'p yo'se'f!

—R. S. THAIN.

Negro Heroism

A few weeks ago, in Los Angeles, when the St. George Hotel was destroyed by fire, and the elevator boy in fright forsook his post, Julius Malone, the house engineer, a respectable colored man, rushed to the elevator and, notwithstanding the warnings of the officers, he ran the elevator up to the top floor and brought safely down fifteen frantic, shrieking persons. On the descent he saw a woman with a child standing helplessly on the fifth floor, and although the elevator shaft was now a mass of flames, he insisted upon endeavoring to rescue them. But the elevator was stalled between the second and third floors because the motor gave out. Before he could extricate himself he was mortally burned, and died a little later in an emergency hospital, and was honorably interred yonder in Evergreen Cemetery.

And does Julius Malone, a Southern Negro, not occupy a hero's grave? Was it not a Christlike deed? And will he not wear forever a hero's crown and wield a hero's scepter?

60

"I'll Hit It Hard!"

A patriotic young man, reared in poverty and struggle, made a trip down the Mississippi River as a deck-hand on a flatboat. When he reached the Southern metropolis he then, for the first time, heard the voice of an auctioneer as he offered human beings for sale. Looking easily over the heads of those about him, he could see the auction block; and when he saw a beautiful young Negro girl torn away from her mother and handed over to a bestial-looking human brute who had the money to buy her as his own, the young man, with his blood flowing in fiery torrents through his veins, withdrew from the crowd and, lifting his big hand to heaven, he vehemently took a solemn oath: "If I ever have a chance to hit that thing, I'll hit it hard; by the Eternal!"

Let no man honestly register a vow before High Heaven unless he is in earnest. God heard that oath, and immediately began to prepare and use that indignant youth from the Middle West. The way was opened before him—he began practicing law—and in a few years he was an acknowledged statesman. At length they were looking for a man to clearly define the paramount issues before the Republic. He was called to New York, and his memorable utterances at Cooper Institute revealed to the Nation that a new prophet had arisen to lead the children of liberty into the Promised Land. Soon he was the standard bearer of a new party. And one glad day he made bare his strong arm to fulfill the vow of his youth, and in the fear of the Lord he dealt a deadly blow; he "hit it hard;" so "hard" that the shackles fell from four millions of human beings; so "hard" that an institution conceived in hell and fostered by devils tottered from its crumbling foundations and sank into irretrievable oblivion.

The recoil of that masterful blow resulted in his own annihilation, and a broken-hearted and bewildered Nation sobbed at his bier; but Abraham Lincoln must live forever as the apotheosis of American manhood.

O, there is still much to do! God would emancipate all souls that are enslaved by avarice, selfishness, vice, and strong drink. The call of duty and opportunity is heard. Let us answer quickly and obey promptly, and God will work other miracles of liberty in the land of the free and the home of the brave.

www.ingramcontent.com/pod-product-compliance
Lightning Source LLC
Chambersburg PA
CBHW041927260326
41914CB00009B/1206